"If You Can't Stand the Smoke,
Get Out of My Kitchen"

"If You Can't Stand the Smoke, Get Out of My Kitchen"

A Humorous Look at Life, Church, and the Family

by

Martha Bolton

Beacon Hill Press of Kansas City
Kansas City, Missouri

The following pieces first appeared in *Christian Herald* magazine:
    When Your Choir Robe Comes with a Gag
    The Rewards of Motherhood
    Is the Turkey Burned Yet?
    We Two Kings

Unless otherwise indicated Scripture references are taken from *The Holy Bible, New International Version* (NIV), copyright © 1973, 1978, 1984 by the International Bible Society and are used by permission.
KJV—King James Version

10   9   8   7   6   5   4

Dedication

To my sister, Charlotte—
who always encouraged me to pursue writing.
(She started encouraging me soon after
we sang that duet together!)

Contents

Preface

If a vending machine has ever robbed you of both your money and your patience, or a defective shopping cart has ever given you more headaches than service, then this book's for you.

Life is full of little frustrations. From January to December we face our share of traffic jams, department store lines, long waits in doctors' offices, and grumpy people. We have a protection against trials such as these, though. It's called laughter. Once we can laugh about a problem, it no longer is one.

So, as you read through this book, I pray it'll give you smiles and strength, humor and heart, laughter and lessons to help you carry on. After all, the Bible does say in Psalm 144:15, "Happy is that people, whose God is the Lord" (KJV).

Acknowledgments

A special thanks to:

My husband, Russ, who never hesitates to whisper those three little words in my ear, "Don't cook tonight."

My sons, Rusty, Matt, and Tony, who—thanks to my cooking—have had to put up with more smog inside our house than outside.

Our dog, Chipper, who has buried so much of my food in our backyard that his paws have blisters.

To Bob Foster, Paul Miller, Ken Bible, and everyone at Beacon Hill and Lillenas who have never tasted my cooking and have the good health to prove it.

And finally, to all of you around the world who have written in requesting my meat loaf recipe. Sorry, but it's a family secret. I appreciate the fact that your churches are in expansion programs, but your building committees will need to find some other substance to use in the foundation.

Promises, Promises, Promises

O N THE FIRST DAY of every year I make many promises to myself. My most recent list included the following:

I promise to greet each morning with enthusiasm and cheerfulness. (No doubt my alarm clock's wanting to get off my frequent flyer program.)

I promise to get more exercise. Sure, you can find me on a tennis court every day, but the other players are complaining my lounge chair's getting in the way of the game.

I promise to save more money. I'm tired of having my Christmas Club statement arrive each December with a sympathy card to my kids stapled to it.

I promise to keep a cleaner house. Walking the "straight

and narrow" shouldn't refer to the only clear path through my living room.

I promise to be more decisive. Or maybe not.

Lastly, when life's little aggravations come my way, I promise to leave them in God's hands and not worry. After all, time has proven over and over again that those things that we fret about today will turn out to be the very things we laugh about tomorrow.

Checks and Unbalances

F EW PEOPLE overdraw their checking accounts deliberately. Usually it's due to a simple error in addition or subtraction, a deposit they credited more than once, or the 14 missing checks they forgot to enter into their checkbook.

Still, when it does happen, it can be quite embarrassing. Once while trying to cash a check in the drive-up lane at my bank, the teller repossessed my tube, then announced over the PA (and local radio stations) that I was overdrawn. As she passed my check back to me through the three cars on my left, I thought to myself, how could I, a person who keeps impeccable records on the backs of grocery store receipts, be overdrawn?

My first reaction was to argue the fact, but since she had disconnected my microphone, I decided to take my problem inside.

I was sure it had to be a computer error, so while waiting in line inside the bank, I went over my figures again. And again. And again. But I kept coming up with the same answer: the crayola scribbling in my checkbook correctly indicated a $300 balance.

When my turn finally came, I walked over to the teller and explained my problem. She listened graciously, then sent me to another teller who listened graciously before sending me to another teller.

"Can you help me?" I pleaded, handing her my checkbook. "I'm overdrawn and I don't understand why. According to my records, I should still have $300 in my account."

She carefully thumbed through my register.

"You call these records?" she snapped. "Your check numbers aren't even in order."

"Of course not," I explained emphatically. "I don't write them in order, why should I enter them in order?"

She didn't laugh.

"And who was this check written to?" she asked, pointing to the blank line at check number 541.

"I thought you'd know," I smiled.

Again, she didn't laugh. I quickly added, "Look, whenever I can't remember who a check was written to, I merely deduct $25.00 from my balance until I receive my monthly statement. If I find out it was for more, I adjust my balance accordingly."

Unimpressed, she merely walked over to the cancelled checks file and returned waving the check in question.

"Check number 541 was your house payment," she said dryly.

I remained calm.

"That still shouldn't have mattered," I said, "because I'm sure I've overpaid on enough other missing checks to absorb most of the difference."

She lowered her head, sighed, then continued her review.

"Ah-ha," she exclaimed. "I see here that check number 513 was for $86.18, but you only entered $42.18 in your checkbook."

"Oh, that. That was for our marital savings."

"A joint savings account?"

"No. I mean to save our marriage. You see, I bought a new dress at Penney's for $86.18, but only entered $42.18 in the register. I hid the other $44.00 in check number 516, which was actually written for $17.00, but I listed it as $61.00 so no one would know check number 513 was actually for $44.00 more."

"Don't you realize bookkeeping like that won't get you anywhere?" she snapped.

"We've been married for almost 20 years."

"Well, what about your service charges," she continued. "It appears you've never entered your monthly service charges."

"I figured you'd say something if you weren't getting paid. And anyway, I still have my cushion."

"Your cushion?"

"Yes," I replied, confidently. "My June 10 deposit. I never entered it into my register."

"Why not?"

"I like to think I have less money in the bank than I really do. It helps me budget."

"But how do you balance your account at the end of each month?" she asked, slamming my checkbook shut and shoving it back to me.

"I've never HAD to balance it until today!" I grumbled.

"Look," she said. "Our records indicate you're overdrawn $45.00. We'll have to go by those figures until you can prove an error on our part. Now, will you be making a deposit or not?"

I hung my head in despair. It was no use. This hard-line teller was going to believe a lousy computer over *my* records.

"I guess so," I sighed, then added meekly, "Will you take a check?"

. . . Oh, well. At least we never have to worry about God's love coming up short.

The No-Sweat Exercise Program

THE BIBLE SAYS in Ecclesiastes 10:18, "If a man is lazy, the rafters sag."

I think a few of mine are doing just that. It's my own fault. You see, according to my doctor, I don't get enough exercise. Well, actually, what he said was *I don't get any exercise.* But I don't believe he's taking into consideration all the catalog pumping and pretzel lifts that I do each day. And only this morning, didn't I successfully execute a dozen or so standing jacks? (A standing jack is a lot like a jumping jack, only you just clap.)

So, it's obvious he's being picky. Nonetheless, I did agree to embark upon a more vigorous exercise program. I've begun taking daily walks (I've got to get my mail anyway). I even looked into an aerobics class. (I looked in and said no way could I put my body through all that!)

But I know I'll get into shape. It's just a matter of working up to it. I'll do a little exercise today, a little more tomorrow, and before I know it I'll be able to put a quarter in a heart-rate machine and not have the alarm go off. After all, my body is His temple, but I'm responsible for its upkeep.

Trouble à la "Cart"

Progress has hit the supermarts.
They all have scanners, just for starts
But when will we
Be blessed to see
A store improve their shopping carts?

You probably already know this, but God did not create the shopping cart. He's a loving God. The shopping cart was man's invention.

Shopping carts stick together, and it's virtually impossible to pry them apart short of using dynamite. Once in awhile you can find a free-standing one, but it's usually stranded in the fruit section with a limp that lets everyone nine aisles over know it's coming.

You may be tempted to go ahead and use the limpy cart, but I've had experience in this area and should warn you. It is a fact that limpy carts tend to get worse the longer you shop. They can adequately handle one box of Ritz crackers, but they fall apart under any additional strain. You'll end up pushing the crippled cart backward at an angle through the rest of the store. By the time you've completed your shopping, the cart will have lost two wheels and nearly a third, and you'll find yourself carrying *it* to the checkout stand.

There are carts with worse problems—like the "confused cart." That's the one with wheels that spin at 180 revolutions per second (each one going in a different direction). What I love to do when I get a cart like this is find a secluded aisle, give the cart one good, strong push, then stand back and watch it shimmy itself to death.

Having the wheels of your cart lock up on you is another memorable experience. However, this only seems to happen in the frozen food aisle where the icicles are already starting to form on your shopping list.

Have you noticed, though, that these same carts have no problem whatsoever rolling around in the parking lot? The minute they make it through those automatic doors, they take off at light speed with or without you. One taste of freedom and they're history.

Now, you may wonder if you should go ahead and let your cart roll off to a new life, but you can't. The law states emphatically that you must leave the shopping cart on the store premises. There's a reason for this law. It's so we can rest assured this same shopping cart will be there waiting for us the next time we go shopping. It'll be there where it always is—blocking the only available parking space.

Yet, even when a limpy cart crosses our path, God can give us the strength to just keep rolling along.

22

When Your Choir Robe Comes with a Gag

I'M NOT what you would call musically talented. Six years of piano lessons only yielded me finger cramps and a signed complaint from our neighbors.

Voice lessons didn't help much either. Oh, I was allowed to join the choir at church, but I had to face the opposite direction. And yes, our conductor did give me a solo once, but unfortunately, it came at the exact moment the entire congregation got up to get a drink of water. So to this day, I don't know if I was any good or not.

What's frustrating about all this is that I come from a family of gifted musicians. My brother can make the piano keys talk. I only make them whine. One of my sisters is a lovely alto, another is a beautiful soprano, another can harmonize with the best of them. I, on the other hand, have been told my best range is mime.

But I've always loved the story of the talents Jesus told in Matthew 25. Whether the workers got five talents, two, or one, the owner's point was to put them to use. The first time I heard that story, it made a great impact, and I determined that whatever talents I've been given (which was the topic of many local debates) would be used for the Lord.

If they asked me to play the piano, I was going to do it. If they asked me to lead a children's choir, I'd say, "When do I start?" If they asked me to sing at our annual church camp, I'd be up at the microphone in a second—even if it was just to keep the bears away. Above all else, I wanted to be willing.

But they didn't ask me to play the piano, or lead a choir, or be the church bear repellent. What they did ask me to do was direct the Christmas play.

"The what?"

"The Christmas play," my pastor explained. "As a matter of fact, why don't you write one for us?"

He said that because he knew I enjoy writing, and he also figured it'd keep me too busy to practice for any more solos.

So for once I didn't even think about all the musical talents I had to offer the Lord. I merely did what my pastor asked: I wrote a Christmas play. And I loved it! Better yet, the audience seemed to love it. They laughed. They cried. (Of course, they used to cry whenever I sang too, but that was different.)

Now there was no stopping me. I volunteered to write everything from the church newsletter to Mother's and Father's Day programs to letters to our missionaries. Whatever department needed words, I was ready to provide them. I'd take telephone messages for our pastor and deliver them in essay form. Simple attendance records turned into individual theses on church growth. And we had the first visitors' cards that ever came out in hardback.

Had I, at last, found something I could do? Had the Lord finally given me a talent?

No, it was always there. I was just so busy comparing myself to five-talent and two-talent people I didn't think He could do anything with my one.

But I was wrong. See, that's the beautiful thing about God's family. We're all needed. Some to sing, some to play the piano, some to teach, and some to write.

Oh, but don't get me wrong. I haven't given up on my singing. In fact, choir practice is Thursday night, and I plan on going.

Now if I could just get someone to tell me where they're meeting . . .

You'll Know It's Love When . . .

Romance is changing with the times.
I'm not sure what it lacks,
But love letters written in the sand
Are now just sent by fax.

We could all use a little more love in our lives. But just so you'll know, it's true love when:

—You think about her day and night . . . not only when your Teleshopper bill comes due.

—You leave him notes that say more than, "The dog ate your dinner. You owe him one."

—You feel as though you're walking on air, and it's not because you put extra Odor-Eaters in your shoes.

—You whisper more romantic things in his ear than, "Charge this on VISA, dear. I think we're over our limit on MasterCard."

—You give her candy that's NOT from your church softball team's fund-raiser.

—You get a tingly feeling all over, and it's not just your Ben Gay activating.

—Your heart skips a beat, even when you haven't eaten Cajun cooking.

—He wants to hold your hand because he's in love, not just to steady himself while he gets a blood test or an IRS audit.

—But you really know it's love when you're sitting in that special booth at that special restaurant, he looks tenderly into your eyes and pops that BIG question, "Sweetheart . . . did you order the Big Mac or the Quarterpounder?"

How to Have a Nice Day—
When the World Has
Other Plans

MOST PEOPLE are basically nice. Throughout our lives, though, we're destined to run into the other kind from time to time.

You know the type—the salesclerk who tells you to have a nice day, then throws your packages at you. Or the bank teller who closes his window just as you get out of line to go over to it. Or the information operator who cuts you off after giving you the sixth digit of your number.

They're everywhere, in every occupation and walk of life imaginable. Like the grocery checker who sees you coming with two carts full of groceries, then decides to go on his break. Or the repairman who says he'll be at your house sometime between eight o'clock and five o'clock, but doesn't tell you which day. And what about the guy who eyes you changing your car's tire on the freeway, then pulls over merely to ask directions to Main Street?

There's also the door-to-door salesman who promises to take only five minutes of your time, then ends up staying for dinner. And how about the bus driver who sees you running toward the bus stop, then waves as she pulls out? Or the lady who cuts in line in front of you, then has the nerve to ask you to hold her place?

We can't forget the guy who dials your number by mistake, then yells at you for not being the party he wanted. Or the lady who compliments your outfit only to add she hopes that look will come back into style someday. Or the loan officer who insists your application is a joke and passes it around the office for laughs.

Lastly, there's the guy in the elevator who, after you ask, "Going up?" will answer, "Yes," through the doors after they close.

But we shouldn't let people like this spoil our day. Maybe they just need to see our smile to get theirs working again.

"But, Officer . . ."

I T'S HUMILIATING ENOUGH to be pulled over to the side of the road and be issued a traffic ticket without having some idiot drive past and snicker. So, I've decided not to do that to people anymore, especially now that I've gotten one myself and know how it feels.

For 14 years I had managed to maintain a perfect driving record of no tickets and only one very minor traffic accident. (But it was a godly accident. I ran into the side of a church.)

So you can see, I'm basically a good driver—even if I did flunk my driving test three times.

Actually, my first driving test shouldn't have counted since halfway through the test I ran out of gas. Still, the examiner insisted on failing me. He even walked three paces ahead of me the entire way back.

The next time I made sure I had a full tank, but the

examiner didn't seem impressed with my 16-point turn. It seems most people do it in three.

Parallel parking cost me my third test. I took the side moldings off a Buick before finally getting the hang of it. Unfortunately, it was the examiner's Buick.

My fourth test, though, was a charm. And since then, I have tried to show my appreciation by being a safe driver.

But now my good record has been blemished. You see, recently I was caught doing 63 mph on a freeway. Everyone else was doing 80 mph, so I felt justified. As a matter of fact, the only way I could have driven the speed limit and not interrupted the flow of traffic would have been to drive the shoulder.

So, there I was following the crowd (which, by the way, the Bible says is not always the wisest thing to do). Just like them, I accelerated beyond the speed limit. But I forgot one simple rule of the road: Never pass a cop.

When I looked in my rearview mirror and spotted the flashing light bar behind me, I shook my head in despair and made my way to the side of the road. I had to admit I deserved the ticket. There was no arguing that fact. Still, I couldn't help asking.

"Officer," I began, "did you see everyone else zooming past you doing 80 miles per hour?"

He nodded, but continued writing.

"Well," I pressed, "if they were doing 80 when they passed you, and I was only doing 63 when I passed you, why'd you pick on me?"

"Because," he growled, handing me my ticket, "you're the only one who waved."

"But I Don't Need a Salami in the Shape of Noah's Ark"

FUND-RAISERS. Don't you love them? The other day I had 9 different people come to my door asking for money (10 if you count the man from the gas company).

These days, organizations are selling everything to raise money: cookies, stuffed animals, candles, spices, cheese, calendars, and more.

And most fund-raisers want cash. They won't accept monthly payments, VISA, or MasterCard. Once, I tried talking a kid into letting me put a nut roll on layaway, but he refused.

Then, there are the "athons": the readathons, jogathons, walkathons, shoot-a-basketathons, the you-name-itathons. Actually, a better title for these particular fund-raisers would be the "I-owe-you-what?!athons." You see, the way they work is the donor pledges a certain amount of money per mile, per book, per basket, and so on. More often than not, the donor ends up owing more than he figured on. Like the time I signed up for a neighbor boy's readathon. Don't get me wrong. I'm sure the young lad's education was greatly enhanced by those 486 books he read. But with the money I ended up owing him, I could have paid his way through college.

It's even worse when it's your own children who are selling the wares. At this very moment I am staring at three half-empty boxes of fund-raising chocolate bars. Each box originally contained 30 candy bars when assigned to each of my three sons. There now remains only 15 bars per box. That would mean 45 candy bars have been sold, right? Wrong. *One* candy bar has been sold. We ate the other 44. Now, not only do we owe this organization $44.00 out of our own pocket, but we incurred a $230 dental bill in the process.

But it's OK. If it wasn't for those dental appointments, I never would have known about the decorator candles my dentist's church was selling to raise money for their new choir robes!

"I'm Sorry I'm Not in Right Now . . ."

I thought that it would be just great.
My callers wouldn't have to wait,
Just leave their message at the tone—
The wonders of an answer-phone.

But since I've hooked up this black box,
It's quite a little paradox
That all those calls and calls I thought
That I was missing—I was not!

Everyone has an answering machine these days. No one reaches out and touches anybody anymore. They just leave messages.

I have to admit, though, I've joined the ranks of the

answering machine people. But I can't decide if I'm happy with mine or not. It seems most of my messages are dial tones. Apparently, a lot of people are hanging up on my machine. (Not as many as hang up on me personally, of course, but enough to make it aggravating.)

I have other problems with my answering machine. Like people who call and leave urgent messages, but no name; people who call and leave names, but no message; and other answering machines that call my answering machine with messages from yet another answering machine.

One feature of my answering machine that I do like is the voice-activated recorder. This is great because it allows the caller to talk as long as he or she wants—unlike those machines that only give the caller 30 seconds to leave his message. I don't know about anyone else, but I use up the first 20 seconds just thinking of what to say. Then, more often than not, I'll say something incoherent and there's no way to erase it. Either that, or I'll have to call back three or four times and leave my message in chapters.

After all, what can you say in 30 seconds? It's like trying to fit thelastparagraphofyourchapterinthespaceprovided whenyouknowyouarerunningoutof . . . beep.

Aren't you glad we never have to worry about God not being in when we call?

The Aggravation Vendors

I REALIZE I should have more patience when a vending machine hasn't behaved as it should—like the patience God has with me when I haven't either.

But I've found most vending machines perform beautifully . . . for the person in front of me. Let me drop my money in, though, and the only thing it renders is aggravation.

I've encountered them all: coffee machines that delivered the cup a minute and a half after the liquid, stamp machines that swallowed more of my money than my checking account, and candy machines that made dietary comments by dropping down a pack of Trident instead of the Three Musketeers bar I wanted.

Coin-operated telephones can be unnerving too. But they only act up when I'm lost, I've just walked two miles to the phone booth, and I'm on my last quarter.

The most temperamental of all machines are those instant teller machines at banks. You know, the ones that will only perform properly if you're making a deposit. If it's a withdrawal you're wanting, they pretend they don't know you.

Still, we shouldn't let these types of encounters discourage us. They happen to everyone. Besides, sometimes it isn't even the machine's fault. Like the other day when I wanted to get a cash advance on my bank charge card. I inserted my card, pressed all the right buttons, but the machine refused to give me any money. I tried the transaction again. Again, it refused. In fact, this time it even kept my card. There wasn't a thing I could do about it. I had to admit I was probably a little over my limit, and the machine had every right to chew up my card and swallow it.

. . . But I still say the burp was completely uncalled for.

Take My Autograph ...
Please

WRITERS OF BOOKS are sometimes asked to sign autographs. That's what I hear, anyway.

Personally, at my last autographing session, there were so few people in my line, I could have signed my books in caligraphy. In fact, the only writer's cramp I got was from doodling.

I've tried wearing sunglasses—you know, to give me a more "famous author" look, but so far, all they've given me is a headache from the frames.

And to date, the only place you'll find my footprints is in my patio. (My husband wants me to take them out, however. He claims they're taking up too much floor space.)

Now, I ask you, is that any way to treat someone who's

listed in *Who's Who?* (OK, so it's not the *real Who's Who?* It's just the "Who?")

When you get right down to it, though, it doesn't really matter how many autographs we sign, how many books we write, or how many people are familiar with our name. We're all "somebody" in God's eyes.

"If You Can't Stand the Smoke, Get Out of My Kitchen"

THE VERY FIRST MEAL I ever cooked as a new bride was a dish called "Eggs à la King." I still have the recipe. It's listed on the hospital report.

Obviously, my husband did not marry me for my culinary skills. My cooking's so bad, medflies take one taste and turn themselves over to the authorities.

Over the years I've tried to improve on my cooking. I've purchased cookbooks, attended classes, and even watched Julia Child religiously. It didn't help. Whenever I flip pancakes, the entire household still takes cover. And firemen continue to use my kitchen for training maneuvers.

But I refuse to give up. You see, I believe we can accom-

plish whatever we determine in our hearts and minds to ac-
complish. And who knows—maybe someday I'll even write
my own cookbook and it'll be a best-seller. It'd have to be.
Every emergency room across America would need to keep a
copy on file for the antidotes.

When Your House Does More Traveling than You Do

I'VE LIVED in southern California most of my life, so I've experienced my share of earthquakes. I've heard those news reports saying, "It's eleven o'clock, do you know where your property is?" I've watched my house doing aerobics. And I've gone under the dining room table more often than my family's dinner plates.

Frankly, I don't enjoy the all-too-frequent tremblers. I don't like changing neighbors two or three times in one evening. And maybe it's just me, but I prefer getting a sunken living room the old-fashioned way.

Some Californians, though, are so used to earthquakes, they won't even get out of bed unless it's at least a five-pointer. Anything less than that, they just consider a mandatory massage.

But whatever frightening situations may come our way throughout life—earthquakes, tornadoes, hurricanes, teaching the two-year-olds' Sunday School class—we can take comfort in knowing that our Father holds the world in the palm of His hand.

Take Two Aspirin and Call My Beeper in the Morning

NOW, DON'T GET ME WRONG. I thank God for doctors. But sometimes their waiting rooms can get a little crowded.

I waited in one doctor's office so long, I managed to read through three issues of *People* magazine, two issues of *Newsweek,* and a copy of *War and Peace* before my name was ever called.

And that was only the halfway mark. I was then led to the examination room where the real wait began. I had time to check through all the drawers, count all the tongue depressors, and retie my gown 98 times before the doctor finally appeared. By that time, my 24-hour virus had already run its course. My fever had broken (I could no longer rent myself out as a heating pad), and that queasy feeling in my stomach had subsided (that will teach me to eat my own cooking).

I did have one last symptom, however—cold sweats. But oddly enough, they didn't seem to hit until I was on my way out of his office. Come to think of it, they came about the time he handed me my bill . . .

"You There, Behind the Hymnal"

I'm quite willing to help out.
No request have I denied.
But no one ever asks me
. . . Guess they don't know where I hide.

Do you ever find yourself hiding behind the planter in the church foyer when that three-teacher-short Sunday School superintendent walks by? Or hiding behind a hymnal when your pastor makes a plea for youth camp counselors?

These reactions to appeals for volunteers are quite normal. But just consider where the church would be without volunteers? Where would it be without those giving individuals who help out in children's church each Sunday with no thought of the risk to their hearing. Where would it be without those who'll help with the church newsletter, serve on the telephone committee, or stay behind after church functions to help put chairs away? Where would it be without the ushers, the choir directors, the hospital visitation committee? Where would it be without those unsung heroes who coordinate church potlucks and perform the life-saving task of removing my dish from the table?

Yes, the volunteer is one of the most important people in the church. So, don't risk the guilt (and back pain) that come from sliding down in your pew during such appeals. Go ahead—raise your hand. Stand up on your feet. Step forward and say, "I volunteer!"

. . . They could turn out to be two of the most beneficial words you'll ever utter.

The 1040 Blues

HAVE YOU EVER wondered what it is about tax filing that makes perfectly normal, well-adjusted people turn into manic-depressives between the 1st and 15th of April? Frankly, I don't believe it's a fear of paying taxes as much as it's the fear of filing. It's called "receipt-o-phobia," and it is a disease. The symptoms include stomping on one's calculator, eating 1040 forms, and playing Ding Dong Ditch at local IRS buildings.

Filing taxes isn't easy. That "subtract line 5A from 10C then add the total of lines 17 and 21, and multiply that by your age" can give anyone a headache. This is why I always let a professional prepare my income tax return.

Each year I gather all my income tax papers and receipts, dump them in a U-haul, and drive over to his office. The conversation between us is always the same:

"Any undeclared income?"

"I won a free cheeseburger at Wendy's last August."

"Any losses?"

"$1.40 in a stamp machine at the post office."

"How about a hospital stay?"

"OK, but will they let us continue working past visiting hours?"

"An inheritance?"

"Don't you just charge a fee like most accountants?"

"How about your dependents? Have any of them changed their place of residence?"

"No. They still live on the telephone."

This routine will continue until sometime before midnight April 15, I've successfully filed my taxes for yet another year.

. . . Or mailed in my wallet, whichever is easiest.

If I'm Still Asleep, This Must Be Monday

INTO EVERY YEAR 52 Mondays must come. You know Monday—that weekly speed bump of life. That traditional day of the blahs.

If you're like me, you have a difficult time waking up on Monday mornings. Your eyelids feel as though they're stuck together with Velcro; and even after you manage to crawl to the breakfast table, you end up using your sweet roll for a pillow.

At work, things get even worse. You find yourself doing silly things like stepping onto the elevator and asking who moved your desk. Or putting your report in the cafeteria microwave and filing your Lean Cuisine. No matter what you try, you just can't seem to snap out of it. You'd like to be left alone to go back to sleep, but your fellow employees need you to get off the copy machine so they can use it.

Mondays are also the day when you'd prefer skipping your exercise class, but your instructor says if you get off your schedule now, you will never work up to that second push-up.

It also seems you're confronted with more of life's aggravations on a Monday—bank lines are longer, traffic jams seem a little worse, and people tend to be less patient.

But don't fret. After all, God said He'd be with us always, and always includes Mondays.

Just like Home Cooking

HAVE YOU EVER had the urge to try a new place to eat, then regretted it the minute you walked through their doors? I made this unfortunate mistake one day while driving with my husband. The only reason the little cafe caught my eye in the first place was because of all the big rigs parked out front. Usually, that's a sure sign of a good eating spot. ... How was I to know they belonged to the waitresses?

When we entered the restaurant, the first thing I did was look around for their health permit. (I like to check up on these kinds of things, especially in places where the windows are so dirty that the cook writes the specials of the day on the glass with his finger.)

It took me a while to find their permit, but I finally spotted it. It was behind a faded, old quarantine notice, but so much food had been thrown at it, I couldn't read the expiration date.

"Smoking or nonsmoking?" the hostess asked impatiently, as she grabbed two gravy-coated menus from off the counter.

"I think it's too late for a choice," I said, fanning away the smoke so I could see her.

"Oh, this just means another order's up," she said, then led us to our seats, handed us the menus, and disappeared into the dense clouds.

Oddly enough, everything on the menu looked pretty good. Oh, you could tell the pictures had been touched up, and seeing the telephone number of the Poison Control Center listed by their dinner entrees wasn't thrilling; but I tried to be objective.

"So, what'll ya have," growled a middle-aged woman as she approached us dressed in a black leather jumpsuit and an apron fastened on with metal chains.

"You must be our waitress," I smiled.

She nodded.

"That's an interesting tattoo," I remarked. "How'd they get it so close to your eyes?"

"Without anesthesia," she snarled. "Now, what'll it be?"

I could tell she wasn't in any mood for small talk, so I meekly gave her our order.

"We'll take two meat loaf platters, please."

I wasn't sure she could hear me over the cheers coming from the kitchen, so I repeated our order. She wrote it down, blew a bubble with her chewing gum, turned, and walked away.

My husband and I looked at each other, bowed our heads, and started saying grace. We figured it would take about 20 minutes before our order arrived, and there wasn't a second to lose!

... And We Don't Even Get Stamps

TIMES CHANGE, and it's not always for the better. For one thing, I'm not fond of self-serve gasoline stations. It always takes me 15 minutes to maneuver the nozzle off the pump because the guy before me left the hose tied in eight double knots. Then, once I untie it, I have to twist it, turn it, yank it, and pull it until I finally manage to get it to pump— at seven-cent intervals. The only time I can get it pumping faster than that is when I lift the nozzle out of the car to see what the problem is. Then, it spills a gallon and a half in four seconds flat.

Pumping my own gas isn't the only thing that time has changed. It's been so long since someone's checked under the hood of my car, it's rusted shut. And these days, the only way I can get my windshield cleaned at a gas station is if I back out over the fire hydrant.

The prices have changed too. Can you believe the cost of today's fuel? I remember the good ol' days when one dollar's worth of gas would take me anywhere I wanted to go. Not anymore. Last week I pulled into a full service island and asked the attendant for a buck's worth of gas. It was just enough to get me over to the self-serve island for more.

But isn't it nice knowing that no matter what changes around us—whether it's prices, service, politics, or fads—God never changes.

You Know It's Mother's Day When . . .

MOTHER'S DAY is that special day when we show our mothers how much they're loved. You'll know it's here when:

—A delivery man appears at your door with a dozen red roses, and he's not lost.

—Your children tell you how wonderful you are, and they're not setting you up for an allowance increase.

—You get served breakfast in bed. (Up till now the only way for you to get breakfast in bed was to sleep with a Twinkie under your pillow.)

—You notice your kids are hiding a card behind their backs, and it's not report card day.

—Your eldest son, the college student, appears at your door; but today, the little bundle in his hand is for you, not your washing machine.

—Not one of your kids asks you to drive them anywhere for anything. (But since this is the first time in a year you've been able to turn off your car's engine, you find the key has rusted in place!)

—You get thanked for all the little things moms do throughout the year—you know, like cooking, cleaning, helping with homework, saving the universe . . .

—For the first time in months, you get taken to a restaurant where the "catch of the day" refers to their fish specialty, not how well you caught your order as you drove by their drive-up window.

—Your husband promises not to watch any sports events on television all day . . . as long as the game comes in clearly on his two stereos, ham radio, and Walkman.

—But most of all, you know it's Mother's Day when your family tells you what a loving, kind, warmhearted person you are, and no one brought home a new pet!

A Purse of Burden

Archaeologists read ancient books.
Of scrolls and treasures, they converse.
But are they all blind? The greatest find
Is at the bottom of my purse.

Some days, it's difficult enough to carry my own weight around, much less the weight of my purse.

Yes, if today's body builders want a real workout, they should put away their barbells and try pumping my shoulder bag for a while. Frankly, everything I could possibly need is in my purse. And a few things I don't need. Here's a brief inventory:

—One shopping list from June '82

—Seven stamps (formerly 14, but they've stuck together)

—The gas bill I thought I paid

—The deposit I thought I made
—The credit card I reported lost
—One individual jelly packet from McDonald's, empty
—One jelly-coated wallet
—One jelly-coated mirror
—One jelly-coated package of Certs
—Sixty-four loose coupons (63 of which have expired)
—One coupon organizer, empty
—A can of hairspray (Now, I know what that hissing noise was every time I shut my purse.)
—An open safety pin (discovered the hard way)
—28 pennies (Obviously, I had just closed my savings account.)
—Eighteen paper clips strung together like a necklace
—A necklace tangled up like paper clips
—And finally, the set of keys that had disappeared in there six months ago

But I don't mind that my purse is well-equipped, ready for any emergency, instant in season and out. . . . I just wish airplanes wouldn't lose so much altitude whenever I'm on board with it.

A Hiding Place

WHY IS IT on those mornings when you oversleep and have 15 minutes to get the kids to school, nothing seems to go right?

I recall one morning in particular when this happened. I found myself racing to my sons' bedrooms. Pausing briefly in each doorway, I tenderly smiled upon their sleepy innocence, then lovingly yanked off the covers and whispered, "GET UP AND GET OUT OF BED! YOU'RE LATE FOR SCHOOL!"

Trusting them to dress themselves, I hurried to the kitchen to burn, I mean, cook breakfast. After five minutes and two more announcements, though, I still didn't hear the sounds of busy little feet scurrying to get dressed.

"You'd better be out of bed," I warned as I returned to check on their progress.

They were out of bed all right but had fallen back to sleep in the shirt drawer.

"You have exactly two minutes to dress and eat," I ordered. "I'll be waiting for you in the car."

"You're not taking us to school like that, are you?" questioned my eldest son, Rusty.

"No one will see me," I assured him, repinning a curler.

"But there's green crud on your face."

"It's not crud. It's an herbal mask, and I don't have time to take it off. Now hurry!"

Grabbing the keys off the table, I went outside to start warming the car's engine.

Moments later, my middle son, Matt, a first grader at the time, appeared in the doorway.

"The Superman cape goes," I said, snatching it from his shoulders as he hopped into the car.

Rusty followed next and passed inspection.

Then, Tony, the youngest, appeared, but for some reason looked taller than usual.

"Why are you wearing skates?" I inquired, glancing down at his feet.

"I can't find my shoes," he shrugged.

Biting my lip, I turned off the motor and ran back inside the house to look for his shoes, or for that matter, any shoes without wheels; but the only matching pair I could find were bronzed. While I contemplated cramming his feet into those, Matt honked the car horn, signaling he had found Tony's shoes under the front seat of the car.

At last, we were ready to go, and it was a race against the clock. We arrived at the school with only three minutes to spare. I quickly handed out lunch money and kisses, but by the time I got to the last child, I was short 35 cents.

Emptying my purse onto my lap turned up seven more pennies and the Sears catalog I had been looking for. A quick check in the ashtray netted another nickle and four rusted bobby pins. Hauling the carseats out onto the curb uncovered three more cents and a video game token.

"Why don't we just borrow the money from the principal?" Rusty suggested. "He's coming this way."

I quickly hid under the dashboard, hoping he'd think the boys drove themselves to school. But it didn't work. He knew I was there and wanted to know why my carseats were blocking the school bus. I explained I was looking for lunch money. He graciously gave me the change I needed, then helped me put the seats back in the car.

Thanking him for his kindness, I sent the boys off to their classes and pulled away. All I wanted to do was go home. The sooner, the better. But I only made it as far as the corner before running out of gas.

As I sat there stalled in the middle of the street, I wanted to cry, but the green crud on my face wouldn't give.

It was starting to rain now, and there was only one thing I could do. I had to gather up what little dignity I had left and start walking toward the nearest gas station.

But then again you can only look just so dignified hauling a gas can down the main street of town in curlers and Mickey Mouse pajamas with the feet in them.

At times like this, isn't it nice to know we can hide in His love?

The Rewards of Motherhood

MOTHERHOOD has its rewards. First of all, children provide you with a free fitness program. You get to run obstacle courses around their toys. You get to do stretches across their bed to retrieve that English book they hid behind it. And you get to do 25 shoulder twists just trying to see around them in front of the bathroom mirror.

Motherhood lets you set your own hours too. You can choose to work the 28-hour day or the 30-hour day. It's up to you.

You also get to meet new people—like the history teacher who wanted to know why on a test your daughter wrote that she wasn't sure who George and Martha Washington were, but thought they worked in the school cafeteria.

You get to travel. You get to drive to soccer practice, piano lessons, school basketball games, orthodontist appointments, PTA meetings, Little League . . . and that's just on Monday.

You get to become a "whodunit" sleuth as you solve such mysteries as who left the glass of milk behind the sofa, and what did they plan on doing with the tree that was now growing out of it.

You can gain valuable judicial experience as well as you determine, through the testimony of witnesses, whose turn it is to do the dishes, whose turn it is to take out the trash, and who's night it is to have control of the television set.

A free telephone answering service is also provided. Never again will you have to run to answer the telephone. As a matter of fact, never again will it be for you.

You get free on-the-job medical training too. You'll learn how to mend both a skinned knee and a broken heart.

And you get a free accounting service. If you forget how many weeks you're behind in your child's allowance, or how much you borrowed from his piggy bank last month, he's got it totaled down to the last penny and will gladly send monthly statements.

But that's not all the rewards of motherhood. You also get priceless gifts—like Mother's Day cards with their handprints drawn on them, or Christmas ornaments adorned with their photograph.

Motherhood also offers a terrific stress reduction program. It's called "hug therapy," and somehow children seem to know how to provide it at precisely the right moments.

You get great job security, too, for no matter how much growing up your children do, you'll always be "Mom."

But most importantly, motherhood brings plenty of job satisfaction from knowing you've done the best you can to mold, shape, and give direction to those lives that God has placed in your care.

Yes, motherhood does have its rewards. And they're unending.

You Know It's Father's Day When...

Dads. Where would we be without them? And that's precisely why Father's Day was started. To give us a special day to tell them how much they're loved and appreciated.

But just so the day won't slip past you, you'll know it's Father's Day when:

— Your son brings you your robe and slippers, and it's not so you won't feel the draft coming from the window he just broke.

— Your wife serves you breakfast in bed, and it's not because the firemen are still cleaning up in the kitchen.

—For once you get to be in charge of the television set, and you're positive you would have been given that honor even if the picture tube hadn't gone out.

—Your daughter tells you what a gentle, kind, understanding father you are, and it has nothing to do with the fact she came home a half-hour late on her curfew last night.

—Your wife brings you your newspaper *before* she cuts out all the articles she wanted.

—Your family gives you a new wallet, and it's not because your old one has too many of their fingerprints on it.

—You get taken out to dinner, and you don't even have to pay. (Your family arranged ahead of time to have the bill put on your Diner's Club account.)

—Your son pledges to take care of mowing the lawn for you for the rest of the year. And you even get to pick which Saturday he does it.

—But you really know it's Father's Day when your kids give you something you've been dreaming about, something you've hoped for, something you've been wanting for a long time, but haven't been able to get your hands on—your car keys!

When the Warranty Expires, Get Out the Pliers!

THE WARRANTY on my refrigerator will soon expire, so I have the repairman on stand-by. It's behaved beautifully all these months, but as soon as its protection is lifted, I have a feeling it's going to start acting up. And to be perfectly honest, I don't want a malfunctioning refrigerator ruining all my family's food. That's my job.

My washing machine worked fine until its warranty expired last year. Then, whenever I placed more than three towels in it, it got the unbalanced load syndrome and would end up doing more shaking than California.

Appliances aren't the only things that play this little warranty game. Automobiles play it too. I found while my own car was under warranty, it could pass all the other cars on the road with ease. Once the warranty expired, it could still pass all the cars on the road, but it had to do it from the back of a tow truck.

Aren't you glad, though, that we never have to worry about the warranty on God's promises expiring? They come with the best guarantee of all—forever and always . . . whichever comes first.

Pass the Hankie, Please

I ALWAYS CRY at weddings. Considering the price of a wedding gift these days, it seems like a natural thing to do.

Yet, that's nothing compared to all the crying the happy couple's parents end up doing. Weddings can be expensive. There are the invitations, the wedding gown, the tuxedoes, the decorations, the flowers, the reception, and of course, all the aspirin. No wonder a wedding ceremony is no longer looked upon as an act of losing a child, but as one of gaining two more mortgages, three personal loans, and a foreclosure notice from your local photographer.

And who can keep a dry eye during the traditional exchange of vows—you know, "For better, for worse; for richer, and when the credit card statements come due; in allergy season, and in health; forsaking some televised basketball games for as long as *they* both shall live"?

Yes, matrimony truly is beautiful. Especially in a day of multiple marriages—where some people have seen more rice than Uncle Ben—it's heartwarming to witness a couple who are in love and who realize that the words, "I do," shouldn't need a rewrite.

Budget Air Travel (or) Only Three to a Seat, Please

OVER THE YEARS I've discovered there's a definite difference between going first-class and flying budget.

For one thing, first-class passengers have plenty of legroom. If a budget passenger wishes to stretch out his legs, he has to get permission from everyone four rows in front of him.

Then, there's the food—another big difference. First-class passengers are given a full seven-course meal. Budget passengers can have a seven-course meal too—six grapes and a honey roasted peanut.

For entertainment first-class passengers get to watch a current motion picture while in flight. The only entertainment a budget passenger gets to see is the kids fighting in the seats next to him.

First-class passengers get magazines like *Money* and *Time* to read. Budget passengers get to read the emergency instructions.

First-class seats recline to offer maximum comfort. Budget passengers' seats recline, too, but it's usually because they're broken.

I've decided, though, that it doesn't really matter how I travel—just as long as my luggage doesn't end up seeing more of God's world than I do.

Biting Off More than You Can Chew

I'VE NEVER been much of a health food person. I refuse to eat anything with more roughage than my patio.

I try to stay away from the kind of breakfast cereal that has to soak in milk overnight to get a spoon through it. I'm a soggy cereal lover myself. I hear enough things crunching and popping during my morning stretches.

Granola is another health food that I try to stay away from. I don't mind food that sticks to my ribs, but when it sticks to the back of my tonsils, I draw the line.

I also try to avoid those nutritional snack bars. Some companies claim eating one of these is equivalent to consuming a square meal. And I think I know why. The ones I've sampled tasted like I was eating a 2 x 2.

Still, a diet high in fiber has been proven to be beneficial to one's well-being. And since it is important to take care of the body God gave us, I suppose I'll have to make myself start eating healthier.

. . . I just wish I could do it without getting so many splinters in my tongue.

The Annual Church Picnic (or) "But I Thought You Were Bringing the Paper Plates"

B ILLED AS a time of "good food, fun, and fellowship," the annual church picnic is the highlight of the year for many churches.

"Good food" is an understatement. Most church folks are excellent cooks. And except for that one year when that petition was circulating, I even get to bring one of my famous dishes to these functions. (The pastor never lets anyone partake of it, though. Something about the church's insurance not covering my cooking.)

The "fun" of the church picnic comes in the form of organized games, like the egg toss. I don't enjoy the egg toss because I always seem to get a partner who cheats. (I've checked the rules, and I don't think he's supposed to be throwing six eggs at a time.)

Lastly, but most importantly, there's the "fellowship." The annual church picnic is the perfect place to finally greet that drama director whom you've been avoiding ever since he announced he needed someone to help with the Christmas pageant. Especially, since your husband volunteered you for the job last Sunday when you weren't there.

It's also a good time to get to know your choir director better by challenging him to a game of horseshoes. I do this every year. It's the only time I can get a choir director to say I've got a good pitch.

Yes, church picnics are a much-anticipated event. Yet the most fun comes when they're over. That's because on that other Sunday when your husband stayed home from church himself, you volunteered him to be on the cleanup committee.

In Search of
Roadside Comfort

HOW DOES the road-weary traveler go about choosing the right motel? Well, to begin with, it's important to note there are only two basic kinds of motels sporting vacancy signs today. First, there are the nice, clean, comfortable ones. Then, there are the ones you can afford.

The nice motels are the easiest to spot from the road. They're the ones your kids hang out the car window and scream for as you drive past them.

The affordable motel lacks such curb appeal. In fact, you usually have to look for their bug-infested "CLEAN AC-COMMODATIONS" sign to know you're in the right place.

There are other ways to distinguish the nice motels

from the affordable ones. You may want to watch for these telltale signs:

A nice motel has an olympic-size, heated swimming pool. An affordable motel has two lawn chairs and a rainbird sprinkler.

A nice motel has a telephone in every room. An affordable motel has a notepad and paper airplane folding instructions.

A nice motel offers a king-size bed in a room with a view. An affordable motel offers a ground-floor room with a bed with a view . . . providing you sleep on the top bunk.

At a nice motel, the maid changes the sheets every day. At an affordable motel, the only time they change the sheets is when someone steals the linen.

"Double occupancy" at a nice motel means two people to a room. "Double occupancy" at an affordable motel means another family will be bunking with you.

If you need fresh towels at a nice motel, they suggest you ring "Housekeeping." If you need fresh towels at an affordable motel, they suggest you lump it.

But no matter what kind of motel you stay at, the important thing is that you return home safe, rested, and not entirely broke.

When You Can't Take It with You

HAVE YOU EVER wondered what you'd take if you suddenly had to be evacuated? Now, granted, if you only had five minutes, you'd grab the kids and the pets, and quickly be on your way to safety.

But what if you had a half-hour notice? Or an hour? Or even a half-day? You know, just enough time to be selective. Have you considered what things you'd most want to save? What items around your house do you feel are irreplaceable?

Not long ago, my husband and I tried making our list.

"The antiques should be first on the list," he began.

"Why?" I asked. "My dresses can always be replaced."

He continued, undaunted.

"And our important papers should be next."

"You're right," I smiled. "We can't leave our marriage certificate behind."

"Marriage certificate? I was talking about my *Golf Digest* subscription receipt."

"Well, what about my pictures of Mom?" I inquired.

"This is an emergency. We won't have time to rent a U-haul."

"I'm definitely not leaving my awards behind," I said, emphatically.

"No, we'll take those," he conceded. "But I'm warning you, between them and your fan mail, we won't be able to fit anything else into the glove compartment of the car."

Ignoring that comment, I continued.

"I'm taking my typewriter."

"I'm taking my fishing poles and tackle box," he countered.

"I'm taking my scrapbooks."

"I'm taking my bowling ball."

"I'm taking my collector's plates."

"I'm taking the VCR."

This continued until, at least on paper, we had our entire house loaded into and on top of our car.

"We may have to leave some things behind," I said, realizing if we were to evacuate, ideally we should make it out of the driveway.

We both looked over the list once more.

"OK," we said, finally agreeing on something. "The bill box can stay."

No wonder the Bible tells us to lay up our treasures in heaven.

When the Smoke Clears

SEVERAL TIMES throughout the summer, my husband will request that I barbecue our dinner—you know, take the flames outside for a change.

To be perfectly honest, however, I don't enjoy dining outdoors. I don't like having to make sure my potato salad is covered at all times just because of the flies. I say if they don't like looking at it, let them go fly somewhere else.

Why is it, too, that the only piece of unblackened meat is the one I accidentally knock off the grill and into the dirt?

Still, every so often I'll try to accommodate my husband's request and have a good old-fashioned backyard barbecue. It's a simple request.

. . . And besides, cooking outside does make it that much easier for the firemen to find our house.

Sorry, but the 4H Competition Is Down the Hall

WHEN I SEE MYSELF in the morning, it's difficult for me to believe I was once a beauty pageant contestant. I didn't win. In fact, the announcer scored higher than me. But it wasn't totally my fault. You see, the criteria for the judging was "beauty, poise, talent, academic achievements, and overall likability." Unfortunately, those were my weak points.

I did manage to impress the judges with other qualities. I had that certain "girl next door" look (provided you live next to a kennel), and the cold sore on my lip and the conjunctivitis in my right eye really made me stand out from the other contestants.

I also stood out in the swimsuit competition. I was the only one in a robe.

As I mentioned before, though, I did lose. But I didn't let it bother me. I realize beauty is only skin deep. What's really important is what's in my heart.

And anyway, who knows how it might have turned out if things had been just a little different. Had it been another day . . . Had it been another set of judges . . . Had I put my shoes on the right feet . . .

When Life
Hands You a Line

Folks rush here and folks rush there.
They just can't stop, you see,
'cept for all those times when they're
In line in front of me!

I don't enjoy waiting in lines. I don't like bank lines that extend into the next county, or bakeries that are "Now Serving No. 4" when I'm No. 86.

Grocery store lines aren't much better. I usually get stuck behind a lady with two carts, 492 coupons, a six-party out-of-state check, and a kid who wanted a toy, didn't get it, and is now breaking all the crystal in aisle 6 with his bellows.

Over the years I've learned something about post office lines. The fastest moving one will come to a dead standstill the minute I change over to it.

At the Department of Motor Vehicles, the line I most

frequently find myself in is the wrong line. But I should know better. As a rule, the wrong line is the one that wraps itself around the building 18 times. The right line is usually longer.

Let's face it, at banks, bakeries, department stores, the post office, or wherever there are people, there will be lines. There's no escaping it. Anyway, it's like they say, all good things come to those who wait . . . and wait . . . and wait . . .

You Know You're Having a Good Year When . . .

You KNOW you're having a good year when:

—The school calls to tell you your daughter is passing
   . . . and they're not referring to notes during class.

—You call a place of business and get put on hold to a
   song you actually enjoy listening to.

—Your dollar bill gets accepted in a dollar bill changing
   machine on the first try instead of the 48th.

—The body repair shop that informed you that you're
   overdue for a complete overhaul and in dire need of
   extensive repairs, was referring to your car, not to
   you.

—You managed to save $200 today. You forgot to bring your checkbook with you to Macy's.

—And finally, you know you're having a good year when that telephone call that came while your radio was blaring, your television set was turned up full blast, the children were fighting, and your husband and dog were both howling about your leftovers again, wasn't your pastor.

...And Then Came Plastic Bags

MANY THINGS have been improved upon over the years. Some improvements, however, I could have done without.

Take, for instance, the grocery bag. I was perfectly happy with paper bags. But now we have to contend with the "new, stronger, more convenient" plastic ones. Have you ever tried carrying two gallons of milk in one of those plastic bags? It's awkward, and the cartons tend to bump each other all the way to your car. Lucky for me, my boxboy usually packs my bread in between them as a buffer.

Another improvement I'm not sure whether or not I like is the new grocery store price scanner. It really helped matters, didn't it? No longer do we have to wait while a checker manually enters each price into the cash register. Today, all he has to do is run the item over the scanner 47 times, *then* he manually enters in the price.

Many food products have "improved" by becoming microwavable. But I kind of like this improvement. Now, I can have dinner cooked and on the table quicker than my family can say, "Pass the stomach pump."

... Yet, in the midst of all these improvements, isn't it nice knowing there's one thing that never needs to be improved upon—God's love. It always has been and always will be "just right."

Now I Lay Me Down to Sleep (And Hope the Mattress Doesn't Squeak)

AS A WRITER, I find myself on the road a lot. My hometown requests it. So, naturally, I've become a connoisseur of motel and hotel beds.

I've slept in beds so hard that rolling over gave me bruises, and in beds so soft that I could use the sides of the mattress for covers.

I've slept in big beds, small beds, long beds, and short beds. I've even slept in waterbeds (and believe me, that's the last time I'll go to a motel where the roof leaks).

Still, wherever I sleep, there's nothing quite like returning home to Old Faithful. My own bed has a sort of familiarity to it. It knows me. After all these years it automatically contours to my body—whether I'm in it or not.

I'm equally familiar with it. I know which springs are sprung, where all the sinkholes happen to be, and how far to the edge I can get without rolling off. And regardless of where I go or how many nights I'm away, it never fails to welcome me home with a lumpy hug.

I guess you could say we belong together. We're both out of shape and make funny, little squeaking noises whenever we move.

My Life as a Doormat

PEOPLE INTIMIDATE ME. Over the years I've let so many people walk on me, I feel like an Odor-Eater.

If someone cuts in front of me in line, I'll ask if he's got friends. If another driver nabs that parking space I've been waiting for, I'll not only back up and give her room but also guide her in. It's been so long since I've had the last word, I've forgotten what a period looks like.

I'm the type of person who gets out of the express lane at grocery stores to put my 11th item back only to lose my place to a two-carted shopper who's counting his items by food groups. I've also been known to spend the night at four-way stop intersections waiting until I was absolutely sure, positively confident, thoroughly convinced it was my turn to go.

Door-to-door salesmen intimidate me the most. I find myself buying things I can't use, don't need, and don't want because I can't say no. Like that time I bought styling mousse for the dog of the '90s. (Sure, it gave my dog's coat more fullness, but she couldn't fit into her doghouse for a week!)

Throughout life, though, there will be times to speak up and times not to. May we always have the wisdom to know which is which.

A "Big Foot" Sighting

RECENTLY, while browsing through a local shoestore, the salesman came up to me and said, "If you see anything you like, just let me know." Then, glancing down at my feet, he added, "By the way, we do go up to a size 12."

Now, I'll admit my feet are a bit on the large size (whenever I play baseball, I can tag first and second base at the same time), but I do not wear a size 12. I can comfortably squeeze into a size 8 . . . providing it's a thong.

From as far back as I can remember I've had big feet. In kindergarten while all the other children were making little saucers with their footprints in them, I had to make a serving tray out of mine. And can you imagine how it felt to have the other kids borrow my shoelaces only to use them as jump ropes?

Christmastime was especially insulting. Everyone

wanted one of my socks to hang over their fireplace because it could hold the big items—like guitars.

Finding shoes that fit me has always posed the biggest problem. I mean, when clown shoes give you blisters, it really narrows down your choices. It seems the shoes I like never come in my size, while the ones I don't like not only come in my size but also look so big, they should be opened for tours.

Tennis shoes seem to be the easiest to find in the larger sizes, so it's no wonder for me "dress up" has come to mean a pair of Reeboks with a clip-on bow. Usually, they look pretty nice, but even I have to admit they probably didn't go that well with my wedding gown.

I suppose, though, that I should be thankful for the size of my feet. After all, if it wasn't for that loafer I donated to my church, where would that new Sunday School class be meeting?

Life in the Slow Lane

I DON'T LIVE life in the fast lane. I drive the shoulder. I'm the type of person who gets heart palpitations when lettuce goes on sale.

I don't like fast music. (Lawrence Welk once gave me a headache.) I don't enjoy fast cars either. (I'm happy if my car can go from zero to 60 in a week.)

I'm what you would call "chilled out" (just ask my husband how often I turn up the thermostat). And I "hang loose" too. (If you don't believe me, just look at my underarms whenever I lift them.)

Still, I don't mind living life this way. After all, the slow lane does afford a much better view of the scenery.

And the Total Is . . .

Grocery stores can be expensive,
But there's no need for groans
For I understand they've opened
A lane that gives home loans.

Over the years I've found that taking children grocery shopping with you can be an expensive experience. Your bill can end up being twice what you budgeted, and you won't even know what you've purchased until you get home and unload it.

Personally, my sons have the habit of tossing in so many cupcakes, doughnuts, muffins, and Twinkies, a lady once mistook my basket for the Hostess display.

And then, there's all the ice cream they try to sneak in. The last time I went shopping, they filled my cart with enough flavors to give Baskin-Robbins a run for their business.

Then, there's the cereal aisle, the candy bins, the frozen pizza display, and the soda section.

I have, though, found one advantage to taking children to the grocery store with you. At least you'll know while you're gone your telephone lines will be getting a rest.

When Everything Goes to the Dogs . . .

DID YOU EVER have one of those days when everything seemed to be going to the dogs . . . literally?

One particular day a few years back, I found myself quite attached to a friend's gray Chihuahua. The fiesty little beast wouldn't let go of my ankle. But don't get me wrong. I love dogs. I just don't enjoy wearing them.

However, my friend assured me that even though her dog did, in fact, have his teeth wrapped around my leg, he was much too friendly to ever break the skin. "Actually," she insisted, "it's just his way of saying he likes you."

I've had other dogs "like" me almost that much—like the pit bull another friend once gave me as a gift. He was a great watchdog. All he did was watch me and growl. (I suppose that'll teach me to stand in front of a hungry dog with a bone in my hand. Although, I thought it'd be safe under my skin.) I owned the dog an hour-and-a-half before giving him back.

Even those memories aren't as bad as some of the encounters I've had with stray dogs. As a rule, stray dogs are twice as big as domestic dogs and can usually be found hanging out somewhere between the grocery store and your parked car when you're carrying a bag full of fresh meat.

But whether it's unfriendly dogs or unfriendly people, isn't it nice to know that God has promised He'd walk beside us—even on those days when all we get is barked at?

Have You Had Your Alfalfa Sprouts Today?

THERE'S NOTHING like a salad bar to make you feel good. Not only is it healthy, but it'll make up for that double cheese pizza you had after church last night as well.

Salad bars, however, do have their drawbacks. For one thing, have you noticed the best condiments are always strategically placed 2½ inches beyond the normal human reach? You can still manage to get them, but you have to duck under the overhang while using two celery sticks tied together with alfalfa sprouts to knock them into your plate.

And there's another thing I don't understand. Why are all the dressings kept in 10-inch-deep bowls accompanied by only 7-inch serving spoons?

How they determine what size plate to give you is another mystery. It seems if they're offering three lettuce salads, two pasta salads, 18 different chopped vegetables, and fresh bread, the plate they hand you is no larger than a Barbie tea set saucer. If they're only serving lettuce and croutons, they'll give you a platter.

Still, in spite of the shortcomings, I do love a salad bar. As long as I don't bang my head on the overhang, burn my hand on the hot potato skins, or slip in the bleu cheese dressing that someone spilled on the floor, I suppose it really is a healthy alternative to junk food.

Growing Up in Slow-Mo

CHILDREN GROW UP fast these days. Hopefully, we'll remember to take the time to enjoy them each step of the way. But just so the transition into adulthood doesn't catch you totally by surprise, you'll know your children are growing up when:

— You find yourself still trying to convince them of the importance of a nap . . . only now it's to get them to turn down their radios so you can take yours.

— They still cry when you leave the house . . . only now it's because your wallet's going with you.

— They still like to eat every three hours . . . only now it's at smorgasboards.

— They still like dressing up in Mommy's or Daddy's clothes . . . only now they fit, and you don't get them back.

—But you really know your children are growing up when they still wave bye-bye to you . . . only now it's from the driver's seat of your car!

The Thanksgiving Identity Crisis

SOMETIMES it seems like Thanksgiving is having an identity crisis. Some businesses are so anxious for your Christmas shopping dollars, they completely ignore November's holiday. Horns-a-plenty store displays are crowded out by Christmas wreaths and mistletoe while "Butterballs Roasting on an Open Fire" is played over their PA systems.

I remember how Thanksgiving used to be when I was growing up. People took time for it. They knew the day represented more than pre-Christmas sales. It was a time for coming together and giving thanks.

It was also a time for sharing. My mother would invite anyone she thought looked anemic to join us for the traditional dinner. Her philosophy was "there's always enough food for one more."

There were never enough chairs, though, and so, we'd have people sitting around the table at a variety of levels, on everything from a footstool to a sawhorse. Some would be at lip level with the table while others had their knees in the mashed potatoes.

But it didn't matter. It was Thanksgiving. And while the Christmas season has its gifts and cards to open, my mother believed at Thanksgiving it's our hearts and homes that should be doing the opening.

Is the Turkey Burned Yet?

Each Thanskgiving 'round the table,
We count blessings, one by one;
But we're all mostly thankful
If the turkey comes out done!

Each Thanksgiving families gather around the table to partake of that traditional bird, the turkey.

Now, preparing a turkey isn't as easy as it may seem. You need skill, you need patience, and if you're like me, you need the telephone number of a pizzeria that delivers . . . just in case.

It's been said the only difference between a turkey and a cornish hen is 10 hours in my oven, and I suppose that's true. You see, I don't think I've ever cooked a turkey right. Either it's underdone—meaning when I take it out of the oven, it gets up and walks to the table. Or it's overdone—meaning my smoke alarm starts playing "Come and Dine."

More often than not, it's the latter problem that I have to deal with. I can take a plump, juicy young Tom and turn it into turkey jerky in no time.

I can't exactly pinpoint what it is about turkey that makes it so difficult for me to prepare, but I've never been able to get the hang of it.

Last year, someone suggested I try lowering my oven temperature (I believe it was the fire department). I tried their tip. The turkey took two-and-a-half days to cook. I didn't mind, but my dinner guests hadn't really planned on a slumber party.

The year before that, my mother recommended I cook my turkey in a brown paper bag. I gave that a try, but unfortunately, the paper bag ended up tasting better than the turkey. As a matter of fact, it was the only item anyone took seconds on.

Wrapping my turkey in aluminum foil probably works best for me. It doesn't keep my bird from burning, but at least I don't have to look at it.

This year, though, I think I might try cooking the fowl in one of those plastic cooking bags. That way if it doesn't turn out edible, at least it'll already be bagged for the trash.

But I've decided it doesn't matter how my turkey turns out—whether it's so good everyone raves over it, or so bad my dog runs away until all the leftovers are gone. The important thing is what it represents. Thanksgiving is a day to count blessings, not culinary casualties. And I do have so much to be thankful for: family, friends, health, work, clothing, a home—and especially that little pizzeria down the street that stays open on holidays.

A Pile for Everything and Everything in Its Pile

ONE OF THESE DAYS I'm going to get organized. I'm going to quit writing my appointments on checking account deposit slips. I'm going to implement a better filing system—one I don't have to pole-vault over to get to my desk. I'm going to answer my fan mail before the mailman has a chance to come back and say he delivered it to the wrong address. I'm going to know what's "incoming" besides bills and what's "outgoing" besides money.

I've heard making lists is a great way to get organized. I've tried that, but it seems whenever I make a list, I merely end up rewriting it the next day. As a matter of fact, I've been rewriting the same list every day for a month. The only thing that gets crossed out is the date.

I've also tried keeping a journal of how an average day in my life is spent. This didn't work out either. The only thing I did all day was keep the journal.

Writing little notes to myself and putting them on the refrigerator door is an organizational trick that I'm experimenting with right now, and it seems to be working fine. Of course, I never actually *read* any of the notes, but they sure hide the fingerprints.

No matter what method I use, the important thing is to get organized. After all, if I were a little more organized throughout the year, I wouldn't have so much trouble each December looking for those Christmas gifts I bought on sale and hid in February!

We Two Kings . . .

HOW I CAME TO BE in charge of the Christmas pageant at my church that first year, I'll never know. Perhaps the church staff thought I'd enjoy it. Perhaps they figured it'd be good for me. Most likely it was because I wasn't at the planning meeting.

Whatever the reason, there I was in children's church one Sunday morning handing out parts to 30 aspiring thespians and one aspiring Donald Trump. (He somehow managed to earn a dollar from his parents for every rehearsal he made it through. I tried to get them to work out a similar deal with me, but they turned me down. They said directing the pageant would be a good learning experience for me and payment enough.)

They were right. Directing the pageant did teach me several valuable lessons. It taught me never to underestimate how fast a five-year-old can leap offstage, run down the aisle and into Grandma's arms. It taught me never to assume that both ends of a donkey will move in the same direction. And it taught me to have plenty of Grecian Formula on hand.

In all fairness, the children didn't give me *that* much gray hair. Sure, we had the traditional pouting, crying, and "I want my mother" tantrums. But as the director, I felt entitled to do all that.

We had the usual missed cues too—like the three wise men who suddenly became a duet.

And then we faced the costume dilemma. The shepherd costume was two sizes too small, and the angel costume was big enough to cover the actor plus half of Montana. I should have fired the costume designer, but I didn't want to hurt my feelings. (Besides, sewing has never been one of my strong points. In high school, I made the only gym bag with sleeves!)

The set had its own problems. I won't go into detail, but suffice it to say that had we been doing the battle of Jericho, it would have fit perfectly.

The older children in the cast taught me a lot too. Like how to keep a straight face when they'd suggest giving the innkeeper a Mohawk haircut.

But the pageant did turn out beautifully. The children were charming, and the audience loved them. They must have loved them. So many cameras were flashing, three of the kids nearly got sunburn.

Was it worth it? Was it worth all the rehearsals, all the sleepless nights wondering if the children would wish the audience "RERMY TSIMCHRAS" instead of "MERRY CHRISTMAS" with their letter cards? Was it worth the risk of watching 30 pairs of lips moving during "Joy to the World," but hearing only my voice? (*I* didn't mind taking this risk. But would the exit doors hold up under the stampede?)

Was it worth all the work, the commitment, the frazzled nerves, the late suppers, the earplugs? Yes! Because directing the Christmas pageant taught me other things as well. The innocence and the sincerity of children are refreshing, their excitement contagious. Nothing beats the feeling you get when a girl volunteers to divide her part so the new kid in the play can have some speaking lines. And years later, when I ran into a cast member who, as a young adult, still remembered his lines, I learned never to underestimate the impact a Christmas pageant can make on a young life.

So, don't worry if the ends of the donkey exit on opposite sides of the stage, or if your angel gets lost in his oversized costume. The important thing to keep sight of is what the Christmas pageant is really about—a celebration of the birth of our Lord.

In Search of the Perfect Christmas Gift (or) "I Love It! . . . What Is It?"

EVERY CHRISTMAS I try to come up with the perfect gift for my loved ones. Something I know they need, something I know they'll appreciate, something I know they won't give back to me the following Christmas.

I've gone the handmade craft route. I've knitted sweaters with three sleeves, crocheted doilies big enough to camp under, and made trivets that melted whenever anything lukewarm was placed on them.

I've also tried giving out home-baked goodies. You know, tasty little morsels with the warning, "From Martha's Kitchen." But that didn't seem to work out either. One recipient hung my sugar cookies on her Christmas tree thinking they were ornaments, then blamed me when the limbs broke off. I discovered another family was using the fruit-cake I gave them to keep their Winnebago level. And somehow the fudge I had sent my pastor ended up being used as the church doorstop. (It wouldn't have been so bad, but he asked me to make another batch for all the Sunday School rooms!)

Catalog shopping helped me out with my Christmas list one year. I discovered lots of terrific, hard-to-find gift ideas as near as my mailbox. Unique items like the "Reclinercize Aerobics Video," for those of us who don't mind exercising but would prefer not to have to get up to do it.

A few times I've found what I thought were perfect gifts while shopping in department stores—you know, those places where they defer your payment until February because that's when you'll finally get waited on. But those gifts, too, weren't received with much enthusiasm. (Although, why anyone wouldn't want a glow-in-the-dark combination wallet/melonballer is beyond me!)

So, year after year I've continued my quest for the perfect gift. And year after year I've watched my family and friends sneak my gifts back to the store. I've witnessed them take measures to have my home-made gingerbread houses condemned. And I've seen that one-of-a-kind present I was so proud of finding have five duplicates at the following year's White Elephant Gift Exchange.

But I'm not going to worry about finding the perfect gift anymore because I've come to realize all gifts, large or small, expensive or bargain table, ordinary or unique, are perfect if they're given in the spirit and love of the holiday.

And I know my family and friends are going to feel that love this Christmas morning when they rip open their presents and find my perfect gift for this year—armadillo bedroom slippers!

They can thank me later.

A Christmas Tree to Remember

I HAVE A difficult time selecting Christmas trees. More often than not, I'll pick the one that's got a bad side—no matter which way you turn it. Or I'll select the one that does more leaning than the Tower of Pisa.

One year my tree was so pathetic, you could have stood it upside down and decorated it, and no one would have known the difference. In fact, it looked its best when it was tied to the top of our car. Everyone who saw it thought it was an artificial tree and I had lost some of the pieces to it. Hanging the tree skirt from the middle branch didn't help much either.

Another year I thought we should go the living Christmas tree route. It died before we got it home. In fact, by the time we started decorating it, it was so dry that Ben Gay could have set it on fire.

Yet, even though it was a lot like decorating a tumbleweed, I refused to give up on it. I adorned it with tinsel, garland, ornaments, a touch of angel hair, and a string of flashing lights (well, actually, the lights just had a short in them, but the flashing effect was the same). And you know what? It ended up looking beautiful, after all.

But then, it doesn't really matter how our Christmas tree stands, does it? The important thing is what it stands for.

It Only Hurts
When We Don't Laugh

YES, DAY AFTER DAY, week after week, year after year we're sure to run into our share of life's aggravations. Some appliances will expire the same week as their warranties. Some shopping carts will leave us stranded. And we're sure to have a few banking errors that we can't figure out no matter how many different calculators we use. We'll find ourselves stuck in rush-hour traffic and in grocery store lines that seem to stretch on forever. We'll run across unfriendly people and be faced with situations that test our patience.

Over incidents such as these, we have no control. We can, however, control how we react to them. The Bible says in Proverbs 15:15, ". . . the cheerful heart has a continual feast." And it's true. If we could only remember to look for the mirth in our mishaps, the fun in our frustrations, and the comedy in our calamities, we'd all be a lot better off. God created us with the ability to laugh. He meant for us to be joyful. So, it doesn't really matter if we lose that prime parking space we wanted or if we lose a quarter in that vending machine, does it? As long as we don't lose our sense of humor.